DATE DUE

PRINTED IN U.S.A.

MY GOVERNMENT
LEGISLATIVE BRANCH

by Vincent Alexander

IN GOD WE TRUST

pogo

Ideas for Parents and Teachers

Pogo Books let children practice reading informational text while introducing them to nonfiction features such as headings, labels, sidebars, maps, and diagrams, as well as a table of contents, glossary, and index.

Carefully leveled text with a strong photo match offers early fluent readers the support they need to succeed.

Before Reading

- "Walk" through the book and point out the various nonfiction features. Ask the student what purpose each feature serves.
- Look at the glossary together. Read and discuss the words.

Read the Book

- Have the child read the book independently.
- Invite him or her to list questions that arise from reading.

After Reading

- Discuss the child's questions. Talk about how he or she might find answers to those questions.
- Prompt the child to think more. Ask: What did you know about the legislative branch of the government before you read this book? What more do you want to learn about this branch?

Pogo Books are published by Jump!
5357 Penn Avenue South
Minneapolis, MN 55419
www.jumplibrary.com

Library of Congress Cataloging-in-Publication Data

Names: Alexander, Vincent, author.
Title: Legislative branch / by Vincent Alexander.
Description: Minneapolis, MN : Jump!, Inc., 2018.
Series: My government | Includes index.
Audience: Age 7-10. | Identifiers: LCCN 2017053421 (print) | LCCN 2017055566 (ebook) | ISBN 9781624969362 (e-book) | ISBN 9781624969348 (hardcover : alk. paper) | ISBN 9781624969355 (pbk.)
Subjects: LCSH: United States. Congress—Juvenile literature. | Legislation—United States—Juvenile literature. | Classification: LCC JK1025 (ebook) LCC JK1025 .A54 2019 (print) | DDC 328.73—dc23
LC record available at https://lccn.loc.gov/2017053421

Editor: Kristine Spanier
Book Designer: Leah Sanders

Photo Credits: eurobanks/Shutterstock, cover; Brendan Hoffman/Getty, 1; Ron Sachs/REX, 3; Orhan Cam/Shutterstock, 4; Xinhua/Alamy, 5; Rena Schild/Shutterstock, 6-7; Anna Nahabed/Shutterstock, 8-9 (background); Pannawat/iStock, 8-9 (foreground); kurhan/Shutterstock, 10; Smithore/iStock, 11; Tom Williams/Getty, 12-13; PhotoGQuest/Getty, 14-15; New York Daily News Archive/Getty, 16; Pool/Getty, 17; Jewel Samad/Getty, 18-19; Hill Street Studios/Age Fotostock, 20-21; mphillips007/iStock, 23.

Printed in the United States of America at Corporate Graphics in North Mankato, Minnesota.

TABLE OF CONTENTS

CHAPTER 1

TWO HOUSES

The legislative branch of the U.S. government makes **laws**. It meets in the Capitol Building in Washington, DC.

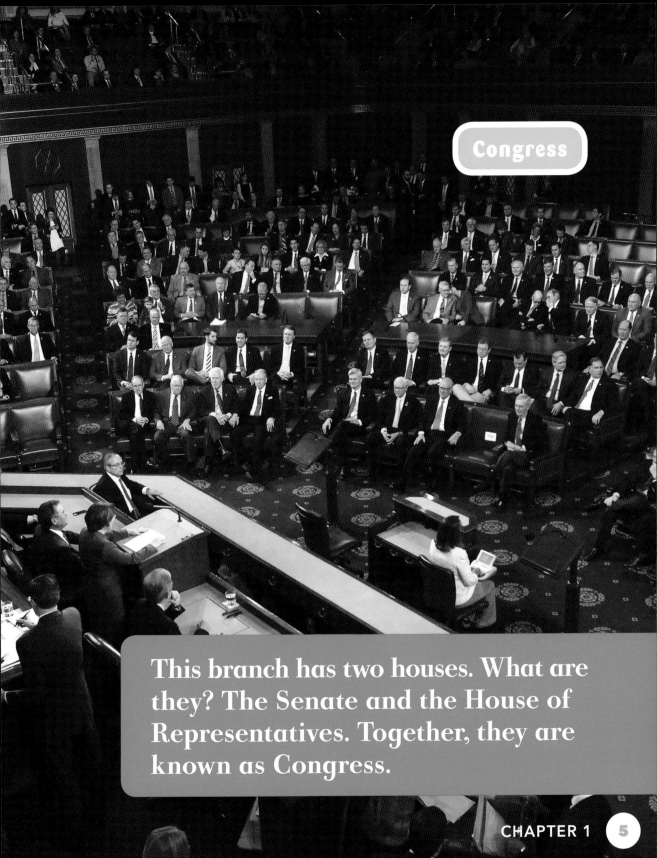

Congress

This branch has two houses. What are they? The Senate and the House of Representatives. Together, they are known as Congress.

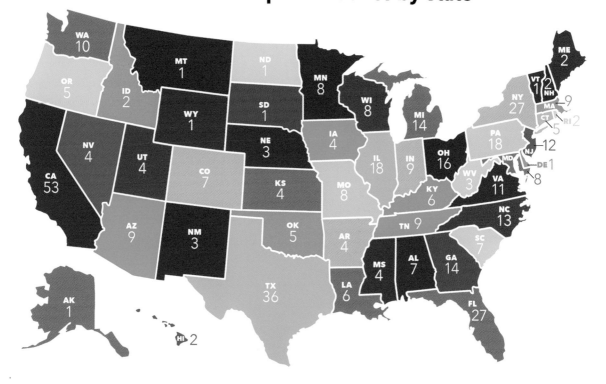

Number of Representatives by State

WA 10
MT 1
ND 1
MN 8
ME 2
VT 1
NH 2
OR 5
ID 2
WY 1
SD 1
WI 8
NY 27
MA 9
CT 5
RI 2
CA 53
NV 4
UT 4
CO 7
NE 3
IA 4
MI 14
PA 18
NJ 12
MD 8
DE 1
IL 18
IN 9
OH 16
WV 3
VA 11
KS 4
MO 8
KY 6
NC 13
AZ 9
NM 3
OK 5
AR 4
TN 9
SC 7
MS 4
AL 7
GA 14
AK 1
TX 36
LA 6
FL 27
HI 2

The House has 435 members. A state's **population** determines its number of members. California has the most. How many? 53. Some states only have one.

Every state elects two senators. There are 50 states. So we have 100 senators.

DID YOU KNOW?

Members of Congress have two offices. Where? One is in Washington, DC. The other is in their home state. Citizens can visit. They tell them their concerns.

Americans wanted to have a voice when the government was formed. Do we need a new law? Should a law be changed? Members of Congress listen to us. Then they make decisions. This is a **democracy**.

WHAT DO YOU THINK?

Why do we need leaders to represent us? What is something you want changed in your community?

CHAPTER 2

MAKING A NEW LAW

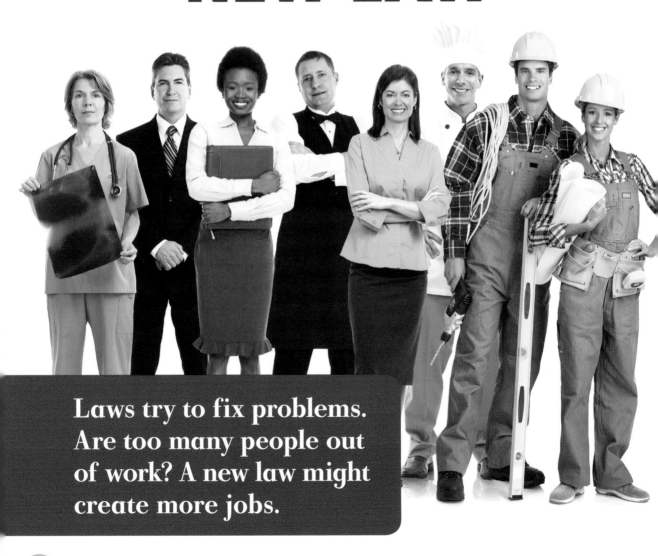

Laws try to fix problems. Are too many people out of work? A new law might create more jobs.

Is something causing **pollution**? A new law might help clean the air or water.

A law begins as a **bill**. A member of Congress introduces it. A committee reviews it. The Senate and the House vote to pass it. Then it goes to the president.

TAKE A LOOK!

How does a bill become a law?

> A lawmaker introduces a bill.

⬇

> Committees review the bill. Sometimes they make changes.

⬇

> The House and Senate vote. Majority votes pass the bill.

⬇

> The bill goes to the president.

⬇

> The president signs the bill into law or **vetoes** it. In the event of a veto, Congress may still pass the bill.

Does the president agree with the bill? If so, it is signed into law. Then we obey it. What if the president disagrees with it? He vetoes it. Congress can **override** the veto. Two-thirds of each house has to vote for it.

DID YOU KNOW?

About 5,000 bills are introduced each year. Only about 150 become laws.

President Johnson

CHAPTER 3

MORE TASKS FOR LAWMAKERS

Congress might disagree with an official's actions. The House votes to **impeach**. The Senate conducts the **trial**. The leader may be removed.

The president is head of the executive branch. He must **appoint** some officials. Senators confirm them. How? By voting. Not enough votes? That **nomination** is rejected.

The president writes treaties with other countries. These are agreements for working together. Senators have the power to approve them. Or they can change how they are written.

Why can Congress do this? For **checks and balances**. This prevents one branch of the government from having too much power. Each branch can overturn decisions made by the other.

TAKE A LOOK!

Three branches form the government. They share power.
They balance power. How?

EXECUTIVE BRANCH

enforces laws

power to impeach;
can override vetoes

can veto bills

appoints judges

can declare presidential
acts unconstitutional

LEGISLATIVE BRANCH

writes laws

approves judges

can declare laws
unconstitutional

JUDICIAL BRANCH

interprets laws

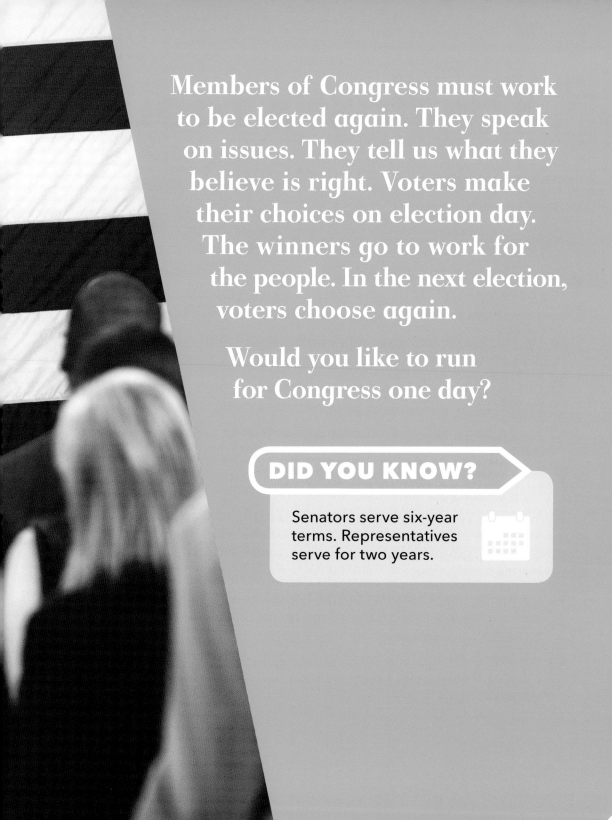

Members of Congress must work to be elected again. They speak on issues. They tell us what they believe is right. Voters make their choices on election day. The winners go to work for the people. In the next election, voters choose again.

Would you like to run for Congress one day?

DID YOU KNOW?

Senators serve six-year terms. Representatives serve for two years.

ACTIVITIES & TOOLS

CONTACT YOUR REPRESENTATIVE

Do you have an issue that might be solved with help from the government? Or do you want to voice your opinion on an issue? Contact your representative.

1. Do you know who your representative is? Find out. Go to https://www.house.gov/representatives/find

2. Put your zip code in the box and click on the search bar.

3. A new page will open that provides the name and contact information for your representative. You will also see a link to his or her website.

4. What do you want to say to your representative? Write a draft of your letter. Make it clear what your issue or opinion is. Ask your representative if he or she can help you.

5. Fill out the email contact form completely. Make sure to include your message in the message box. Ask an adult to help you if you need it.

6. Would you like to request a meeting with your representative? Click on "Request a Meeting." Ask an adult to help you with the form. And make sure to go to the meeting with an adult.

appoint: To choose someone for a job or position.

bill: A written plan for a new law.

checks and balances: A system that ensures one branch of the government is not more powerful than the other branches.

democracy: A form of government in which the people choose their leaders through elections.

impeach: To formally charge a public official with misconduct.

laws: Rules made and enforced by a government.

nomination: A person named for a position or job.

override: To reject or cancel a decision.

pollution: A substance in the environment that is harmful or has poisonous effects.

population: The total number of people who live in a place.

trial: The examination of evidence to decide if a charge or claim is true.

vetoes: Stops a bill from becoming a law.

INDEX

TO LEARN MORE

Learning more is as easy as 1, 2, 3.

1) Go to www.factsurfer.com

2) Enter "legislativebranch" into the search box.

3) Click the "Surf" button to see a list of websites.

With factsurfer, finding more information is just a click away.